JAMESTOWN PUB

ENGLISH, YES!
LITERACY

Learning English Through Literature

JAMESTOWN PUBLISHERS

a division of NTC/CONTEMPORARY PUBLISHING GROUP
Lincolnwood, Illinois USA

Publisher: Steve Van Thournout
Editorial Director: Cindy Krejcsi
Executive Editor: Mary Jane Maples
Editor: Paula Eacott
Art Director: Ophelia M. Chambliss
Cover and interior design: Michael Kelly
Cover illustration: Westlight / © David Chamielewski
Production Manager: Margo Goia
Production Coordinator: Denise Duffy

ISBN: 0-80961-1913-1

Published by Jamestown Publishers, a division of
NTC/Contemporary Publishing Group.
© 1998 NTC/Contemporary Publishing Group, 4255 West Touhy Avenue,
Lincolnwood (Chicago), Illinois 60646-1975 U.S.A.

8 9 0 DH 0 9 8 7 6 5 4 3 2 1

CONTENTS

The Alphabet

Capital Letters

A B C D E F G H I J K L M N

O P Q R S T U V W X Y Z

Circle.

A	B	(A)	J	K
E	D	E	F	R
C	C	O	D	G
S	R	P	B	S
R	P	B	R	S

W	X	V	(W)	K
M	M	N	W	Y
T	L	F	E	T
B	R	H	E	B
V	W	Y	V	J

Match.

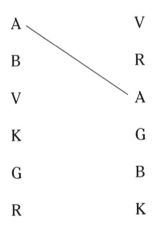

A   V

B   R

V   A

K   G

G   B

R   K

Circle.

T	(T)ELEPHONE	S(T)UDEN(T)	STATE
L	LAST	NICKEL	DOLLAR
I	CITY	SHIRT	TIME
F	LEFT	FRIDAY	FIFTEEN
E	NAME	STREET	TEACHER
K	WEEK	SKIRT	JACKET

Write.

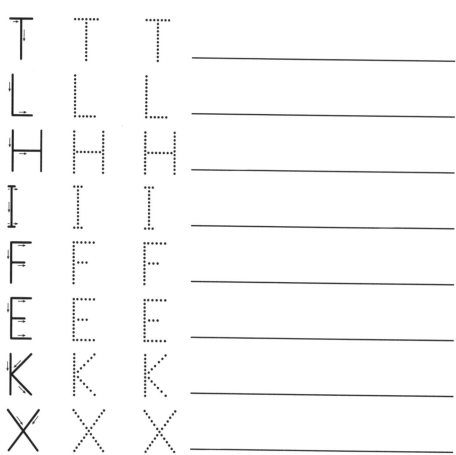

Circle.

V	FI(V)E	MOVIES	VEGETABLE
A	NAME	ART	JACKET
M	MATH	DIME	GYM
N	JEANS	LUNCH	TEN
W	SWEATER	TWO	WHITE
Y	YES	MAY	HISTORY

Write.

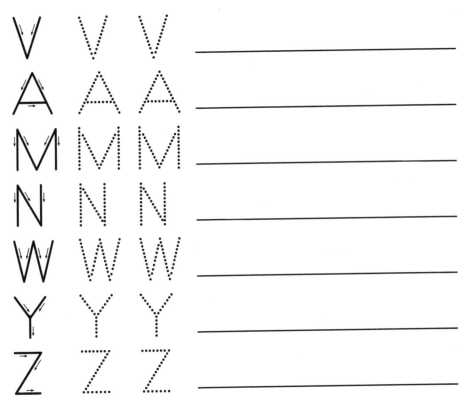

Circle.

C	ⒸLASS	JACKET	BLACK
S	BEANS	STREET	FISH
D	MONDAY	DIME	SALAD
R	NUMBER	RED	LARGE
P	POOL	PANTS	APPLE
B	JOB	BOOTS	LIBRARY

Write.

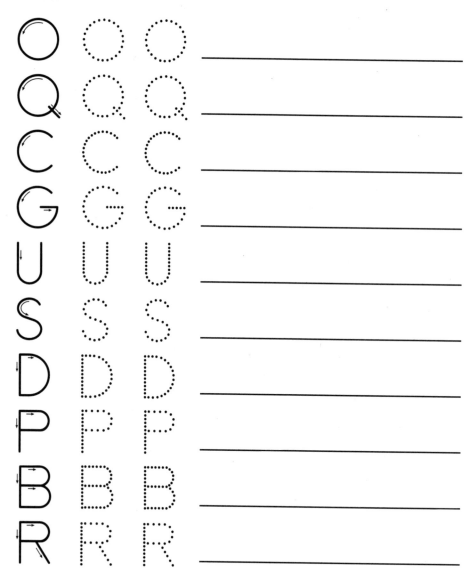

The Alphabet

Small Letters

a b c d e f g h i j k l m n

o p q r s t u v w x y z

Circle.

a	o	a	c	g
f	f	(r)	e	a
c	c	o	d	g
s	r	p	b	s
t	k	l	f	t

n	h	w	n	x
m	m	n	w	y
r	n	r	e	m
b	r	h	e	b
v	w	y	v	x

Match.

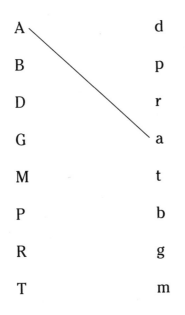

A	d
B	p
D	r
G	a
M	t
P	b
R	g
T	m

Write.

a	a	_____	**h**	h	_____
b	b	_____	**i**	i	_____
c	c	_____	**j**	j	_____
d	d	_____	**k**	k	_____
e	e	_____	**l**	l	_____
f	f	_____	**m**	m	_____
g	g	_____	**n**	n	_____

Complete the words. Write the letters.

bill

 ill

dime

___ ime

nickel

___ ickel

cake

___ ake

egg

___ gg

apple

___ pple

Write.

o	o	_____	**u**	u	_____
p	p	_____	**v**	v	_____
q	q	_____	**w**	w	_____
r	r	_____	**x**	x	_____
w	w	_____	**y**	y	_____
t	t	_____	**z**	z	_____

Complete the words. Write the letters.

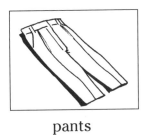

pants

___ ants

shirt

___ hirt

track suit

___ rack suit

rice

___ ice

orange

___ range

vegetables

___ egetables

Complete the words. Write the letters.

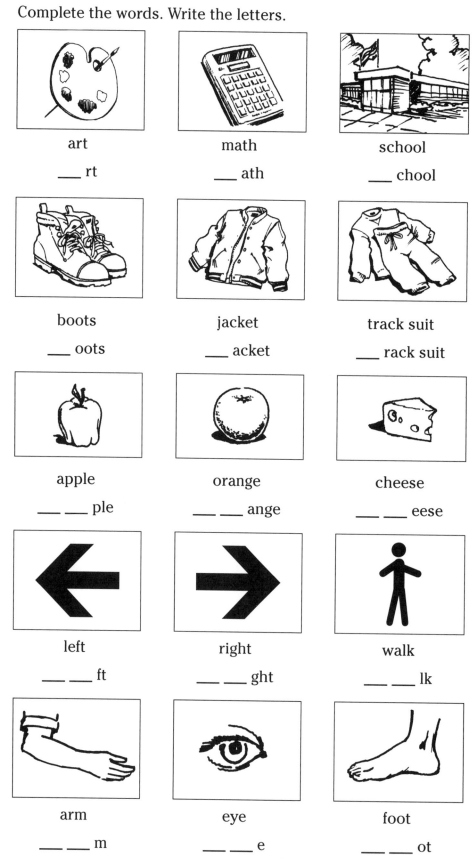

art

___ rt

math

___ ath

school

___ chool

boots

___ oots

jacket

___ acket

track suit

___ rack suit

apple

___ ___ ple

orange

___ ___ ange

cheese

___ ___ eese

left

___ ___ ft

right

___ ___ ght

walk

___ ___ lk

arm

___ ___ m

eye

___ ___ e

foot

___ ___ ot

Write the words.

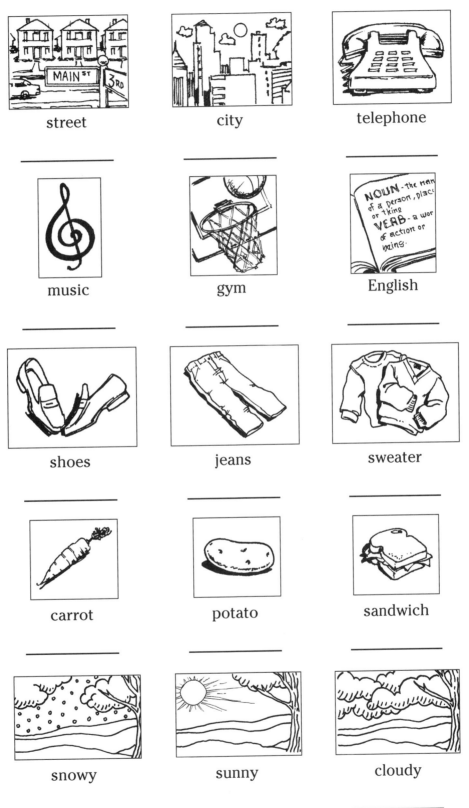

street

city

telephone

_____

music

gym

English

_____

shoes

jeans

sweater

_____

carrot

potato

sandwich

_____

snowy

sunny

cloudy

_____

Numbers

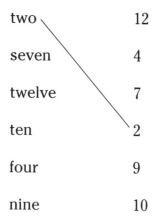

| 1 | 2 | 3 | 4 | 5 | 6 | 7 | 8 |
| 9 | 10 | 11 | 12 | | | | |

Circle.

1	2	3	4	①
2	9	8	2	5
3	8	3	5	6
4	9	8	4	5

6	8	6	9	1
8	7	9	4	8
11	10	12	11	1
12	1	2	12	10

Match.

two	12
seven	4
twelve	7
ten	2
four	9
nine	10

Unit 1

Personal Information

School ID Cards

Horton School Identification Card

Name <u>Ana</u>   <u>Sanchez</u>
     first   last

    Status <u>student</u>

Horton School Identification Card

Name <u>John</u>   <u>Quincy</u>
     first   last

    Status <u>teacher</u>

Student Form

Name <u>Ana</u>   <u>Sanchez</u>
     first   last

Address   <u>123 Oak Street</u>
            street
            <u>Smalltown Iowa 40258</u>
            city   state   zip code

            Telephone number <u>273-9493</u>

Words to Learn

Name Words
name
first name
last name

My first name is Ana.
My last name is Sanchez.

Titles

Mr. Miss Mrs. Ms.

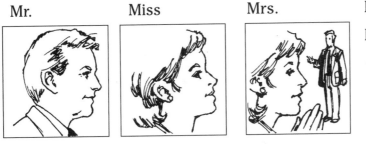

Miss or Mrs.

Note: Use titles before names and last names:
Mr. John Quincy, Mr. Quincy

School Words
student teacher school

Personal Information Words
address
street city state

zip code 60611

telephone telephone number
789-1479

YOU CAN ANSWER THESE QUESTIONS

Put an *x* in the box next to the correct answer.

Reading Comprehension

1. Ana Sanchez
   Her first name is
   ☒ Ana.
   ❑ Sanchez.

2. John Quincy
   His last name is
   ❑ John.
   ❑ Quincy.

3. Ana Sanchez
   Sanchez is the
   ❑ first name.
   ❑ last name.

4. John Quincy
   Quincy is the
   ❑ first name.
   ❑ last name.

5. Ana Sanchez is a
   ❑ teacher.
   ❑ student.

6. John Quincy is a
   ❑ teacher.
   ❑ student.

7. Ana's address is
   ❑ 273-9403.
   ❑ 123 Oak Street.

Vocabulary

8.
   ❑ street
   ❑ telephone

9.
   ❑ street
   ❑ city

10.
    ❑ school
    ❑ state

How many questions did you answer correctly? Circle your score. Then fill in your score on the Score Chart on page 91.

Number Correct	1	2	3	4	5	6	7	8	9	10
Score	10	20	30	40	50	60	70	80	90	100

EXERCISES TO HELP YOU

Exercise A
Finding Words
Circle.

1. FIRST	FOREST	(FIRST)	FROST
2. LAST	LIST	LEFT	LAST
3. NAME	TAME	NAME	FAME
4. first	film	fist	first
5. last	lift	last	lost
6. name	none	same	name

Exercise B
Finding Letters
Circle the letters in Ana's last name.

1. Ana Sanchez

(A) B C D E F G H I J K L M

N O P Q R S T U V W X Y Z

Circle the letters in Mr. Quincy's first name.

2. John Quincy

A B C D E F G H I J K L M

N O P Q R S T U V W X Y Z

3. What letters are in your first name? Circle them.

A B C D E F G H I J K L M

N O P Q R S T U V W X Y Z

Try It
Say the letters.

Exercise C
Practicing Vocabulary: Name Words
Match.

Mark Jones

1. Name ——————— Mark
2. First name ——— Mark Jones
3. Last name   Jones

Linda Lake

1. Name   Lake
2. First name   Linda
3. Last name   Linda Lake

Exercise D
Using Vocabulary: Name Words
Complete the forms. Use the names.

Tom Chang

> Name_____   _____
>   first   last

Julia Post

> Name_____   _____
>   first   last

Try It
Complete the form. Use your name.

> Name_____   _____
>   first   last

Exercise E
Learning Vocabulary
Match.

My name is Fred Smith.
My address is 109 State
Street, Chicago, Illinois.
My zip code is 60006.

Street

Name

State

Fred Smith

109 State Street

Chicago, Illinois 60006

Zip Code

City

Match.

My name is Jane Ames.
My address is 356 Ocean
Street, San Jose, California.
My zip code is 95123.

San Jose

Ames

California

Name
_____
    first   last

Address
_____
    street

_____
city   state   zip code

Jane

356 Ocean Street

95123

Exercise F
Reviewing Vocabulary
Circle.

1. Lily **Lee**   first name   (last name)

2. 575-5790   telephone number   zip code

3. 145 Green Street   street   city

4. 60614   zip code   telephone number

5. California   city   state

Exercise G
Understanding Vocabulary: Telephone Numbers
Complete the form.

My name is Amy Chan.
My telephone number is 789-9419.

My name is Pedro Diaz.
My telephone number is 277-6135.

Name *Amy* _____   _____
          first   last

Telephone number _____

Name _____   *Diaz* _____
          first   last

Telephone number _____

Exercise H
Read and Write
Complete the form.

Name _____ *Pulaski* _____
        first   last

Address _____
            street

_____ _____ _____
            city   state   zip code

Telephone number _____

SHARING WITH OTHERS

Part A
Write about yourself.

Name _____

       first   last

Address _____

       street

_____

       city   state   zip code

Telephone number _____

Part B
Write about your school.

School name _____

Address _____

       street

_____

       city   state   zip code

Telephone number _____

Part C
Write the names of three classmates.

_____

first name   last name

_____

first name   last name

_____

first name   last name

Unit 2

Schedules

A Schedule

Here is Ana's schedule.

	Monday	Tuesday	Wednesday	Thursday	Friday	Saturday	Sunday
8:00 A.M.	math	math	math	math	math		
9:00	ESL	ESL	ESL	ESL	ESL		
10:00	art	music	art	music	art	pool	
11:00	history	geography	history	geography	history		church
12:00 P.M.	lunch	lunch	lunch	lunch	lunch		
1:00	English	English	English	English	English		
2:00	library	library	library	library	library	mall	
3:00	gym	gym	gym	gym	gym		
4:00							
5:00	job		job		job		movies

On weekdays, Ana goes to school.
Her first class is at 8 o'clock.
She has a job on Monday, Wednesday, and Friday.
On weekends, Ana has fun.

Note:
weekends = Saturday and Sunday
weekdays = Monday, Tuesday, Wednesday, Thursday, Friday

a.m. = morning, before noon
p.m. = afternoon, after noon

Words to Learn

Subjects

math

English

art

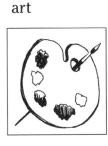

history

geography

gym

music

ESL

Places

library

pool

mall

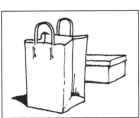

church

movies

Days of the Week

Monday	Tuesday	Wednesday	Thursday
Friday	Saturday	Sunday	

Put an *x* in the box next to the correct answer.

Reading Comprehension

1. Ana has math class at
   - ❑ 7:00.
   - ☒ 8:00.

2. Ana has lunch at
   - ❑ 10:00.
   - ❑ 12:00.

3. Ana has gym at
   - ❑ 2:00.
   - ❑ 3:00.

4. Ana goes to church on
   - ❑ Monday.
   - ❑ Sunday.

5. Ana goes to the pool on
   - ❑ Sunday.
   - ❑ Saturday.

6. Ana's job is on
   - ❑ Monday, Wednesday, and Friday.
   - ❑ Monday, Tuesday, and Thursday.

Vocabulary

7.
   - ❑ history
   - ❑ math

8.
   - ❑ music
   - ❑ geography

9. day of the week
   - ❑ English
   - ❑ Wednesday

10. weekend
   - ❑ Friday and Saturday
   - ❑ Saturday and Sunday

How many questions did you answer correctly? Circle your score. Then fill in your score on the Score Chart on page 91.

Number Correct	1	2	3	4	5	6	7	8	9	10
Score	10	20	30	40	50	60	70	80	90	100

EXERCISES TO HELP YOU

Exercise A
Practicing Vocabulary: Places
Match.

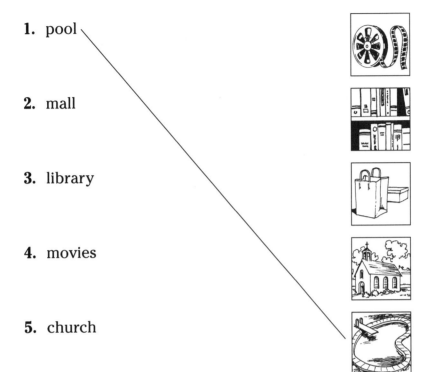

1. pool

2. mall

3. library

4. movies

5. church

Exercise B
Practicing Vocabulary: Subjects
Complete the words.

1. ENGLISH

2. G _____

3. A _____

4. M _____

Exercise C
Learning Vocabulary: Times
Circle.

1. 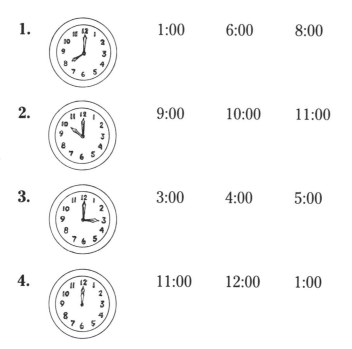 1:00   6:00   8:00

2. 9:00   10:00   11:00

3. 3:00   4:00   5:00

4. 11:00   12:00   1:00

Write the times.

___   ___   ___   ___   ___

Try It
Work with a partner. Say the conversation.

Exercise D
Learning Vocabulary: Days of the Week

Sunday	Monday	Tuesday	Wednesday	Thursday	Friday	Saturday
1	2	3	4	5	6	7
8	9	10	11	12	13	14
15	16	17	18	19	20	21
22	23	24	25	26	27	28
29	30	31				

What day is it? Use the calendar. Circle.

1	(Sunday)	Tuesday	Monday
5	Tuesday	Wednesday	(Thursday)
2	Monday	Tuesday	Saturday
7	Saturday	Sunday	Thursday
8	Sunday	Monday	Tuesday
12	Friday	Thursday	Sunday

What day is it? Use the calendar. Write.

3 _____

10 _____ *Tuesday* _____

13 _____

22 _____

Vocabulary Review

Complete Al's schedule. Use the information in the box.

	Monday	Tuesday	Wednesday	Thursday	Friday
8:00 A.M.					
9:00					
10:00					
11:00					
12:00 P.M.					
1:00					
2:00	gym	gym	gym	gym	gym

Monday,   Tuesday,   Wednesday,   Thursday,   Friday
gym at 2:00   lunch at 11:00
English at 8:00   history at 12:00
math at 9:00   library at 1:00

Tuesday, Thursday
art at 10:00

Monday, Wednesday, Friday
music at 10:00

Exercise F
Vocabulary Review

Write the missing word.

1. Monday, _____Tuesday_____, Wednesday

2. Sunday, _____, Tuesday

3. Thursday, _____, Saturday

4. Wednesday, _____, Friday

5. Saturday, _____, Monday

Exercise G
Read and Write

Yoko's Schedule

	Monday	Tuesday	Wednesday	Thursday	Friday	Saturday	Sunday
8:00 A.M.							
9:00	ESL	ESL	ESL	ESL	ESL	job	
10:00	English	English	English	English	English		
11:00							
12:00 P.M.	lunch	lunch	lunch	lunch	lunch		
1:00	history	geography	history	geography	history		
2:00	library	library	library	library	library		
3:00	art	music	art	music	art		
4:00							
5:00	pool		pool			movies	

Write.

1. Yoko has English class at __10:00__ .

2. Yoko goes to the library at _____ .

3. Yoko has lunch at _____ .

4. Yoko has music class on Tuesday and _____ .

5. Yoko has history class on Monday, Wednesday,

   and _____ .

Read the conversations. Complete Yoko's schedule.

SHARING WITH OTHERS

1. Write your schedule.

	Monday	Tuesday	Wednesday	Thursday	Friday	Saturday	Sunday
8:00 A.M.							
9:00							
10:00							
11:00							
12:00 P.M.							
1:00							
2:00							
3:00							
4:00							
5:00							
6:00							
7:00							

2. Talk about your schedule with a partner. Use questions like the ones in Exercise G.

Unit 3

Shopping

Back-to-School Sale

Get clothes for school at low prices!

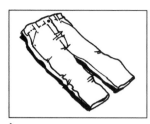

jeans
$22.00
S, M, L, XL
blue, black

jackets
$29.99
S, M, L, XL
black, brown, blue

shirts
$12.00
S, M, L, XL
assorted colors

T-shirts
$9.00
S, M, L, XL
assorted colors

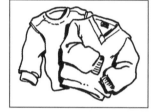

sweaters
$24.00
S, M, L, XL
white, red, blue

track suits
$14.99
S, M only
assorted colors

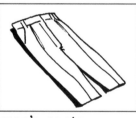

men's pants
$28.50
S, M, L
blue, brown, black

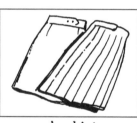

women's skirts
$19.00
S, M, L, XL
blue, green, black

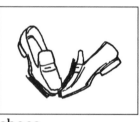

shoes
$32.00
all sizes
black, brown

athletic shoes
$49.90
all sizes
white

boots
$54.99
all sizes
blue, brown, black

Note:
99=ninety-nine
24=twenty-four

assorted colors=
many different
colors

Words to Learn

Clothing

boots	jacket	jeans	pants	shirt
shoes	skirt	sweater	track suit	T-shirt

Colors

blue	brown	black
green	red	white

Sizes

small S   medium M   large L   extra large XL

Money

penny	nickel	dime	quarter
1¢	5¢	10¢	25¢
$.01	$.05	$.10	$.25

one-dollar bill	five-dollar bill	ten-dollar bill	twenty-dollar
$1.00	$5.00	$10.00	bill $20.00

Numbers

thirteen	13		twenty	20
fourteen	14		thirty	30
fifteen	15		forty	40
sixteen	16		fifty	50
seventeen	17		sixty	60
eighteen	18		seventy	70
nineteen	19		eighty	80
			ninety	90

YOU CAN ANSWER THESE QUESTIONS

Put an *x* in the box next to the correct answer.

Reading Comprehension

1. The price of jeans is
   - ❏ $22.00.
   - ❏ $29.99.

2. The price of a T-shirt is
   - ❏ $9.00.
   - ❏ $19.00.

3. $24.00 is the price of the
   - ❏ shirts.
   - ❏ sweaters.

4. Jeans come in
   - ❏ black, blue.
   - ❏ blue, red.

5. Shirts come in
   - ❏ white only.
   - ❏ assorted colors.

6. Jackets come in
   - ❏ S, M, XL sizes.
   - ❏ M, L, XL sizes.

7. The sale is for
   - ❏ party clothes.
   - ❏ school clothes.

Vocabulary

8. Size M means
   - ❏ small.
   - ❏ medium.

9. Assorted colors means
   - ❏ one color.
   - ❏ many different colors.

10. A sale means
   - ❏ no prices.
   - ❏ low prices.

How many questions did you answer correctly? Circle your score. Then fill in your score on the Score Chart on page 91.

Number Correct	1	2	3	4	5	6	7	8	9	10
Score	10	20	30	40	50	60	70	80	90	100

EXERCISES TO HELP YOU

Exercise A
Practicing Vocabulary: Clothing
Complete the sentences. Use words from the box.

boots	shoes
jacket	skirt
jeans	sweater
pants	track suit
shirt	T-shirt

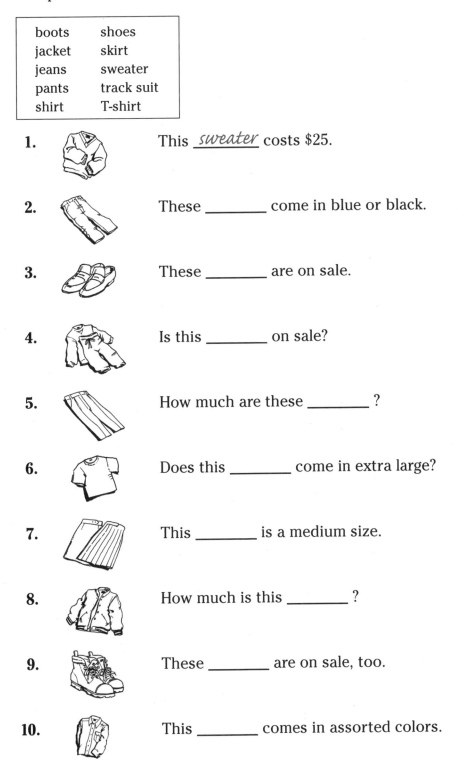

1. This _sweater_ costs $25.

2. These _____ come in blue or black.

3. These _____ are on sale.

4. Is this _____ on sale?

5. How much are these _____ ?

6. Does this _____ come in extra large?

7. This _____ is a medium size.

8. How much is this _____ ?

9. These _____ are on sale, too.

10. This _____ comes in assorted colors.

Exercise B
Practicing Vocabulary: Numbers
Write the numbers.

20   *twenty*

30   _____

50   _____

70   _____

24   *-four*

32   *-two*

65   *-five*

Exercise C
Practicing Vocabulary: Money
Match. Draw lines.

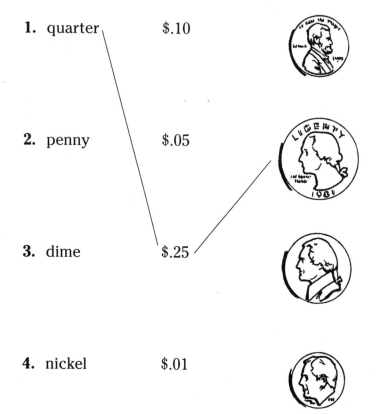

1. quarter $.10

2. penny $.05

3. dime $.25

4. nickel $.01

Exercise D
Circle.

1.

$1.75 $5.40 $1.45

2.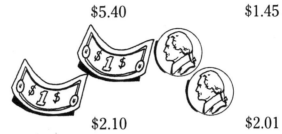

$2.00 $2.10 $2.01

3.

$20.51 $21.20 $21.50

4.

$1.75 $5.40 $1.45

5.

$10.87 $10.78 $10.85

Exercise E
Write.

1.   *$3.25*

2.

3.

4.

5.

Exercise F

Read and Write

Complete the conversations. Use the information in the box.

Clothing	Price	Size
	$35	L

Clothes	Price	Size
	$22	S

Exercise G
Read and Write
Complete the conversations. Use the information in the box.

| jacket $35 | T-shirt $12 | jeans $22 | sweater $24 |

1.

Customer: How much are these _____?

Clerk: They're _____.

Customer: Here's _____.

Clerk: Your change is _____.

2.

Customer: How much is this _____?

Clerk: It's _____.

Customer: Here's _____.

Clerk: Your change is _____.

3.

Customer: How much are these _____?

Clerk: They're _____.

Customer: Here's _____.

Clerk: Your change is _____.

Try It
Work with a partner. Say the conversations.

SHARING WITH OTHERS

Part A

1. What clothes are you wearing now? Make a list.

Ideas:
a T-shirt	a green T-shirt
a jacket	a black jacket
jeans	blue jeans

_____

_____

_____

_____

2. Share your list with a partner.

Part B

1. What are your favorite clothes? Make a list.

_____

_____

_____

_____

2. Talk with a partner. Tell about your favorite clothes.

Unit 4

Food

Food Pyramid

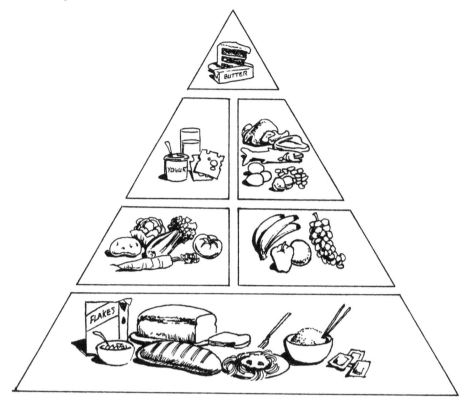

Sweets and fats
Do not eat a lot of these.

Milk and cheese
2–3 servings every day

Meat, poultry, fish, eggs
2–3 servings every day

Vegetables
3–5 servings every day

Fruit
2–4 servings every day

Bread, cereal, rice, pasta
6–11 servings every day

The pyramid shows the right foods to eat every day.

Meals

In the United States, most people eat three meals every day.
1. Breakfast is in the morning. (6:00–9:00 a.m.)
2. Lunch is in the afternoon. (12:00–2:00 p.m.)
3. Dinner is in the evening. (5:00–8:00 p.m.)

Meals often have three parts:
1. soup or salad
2. meat and vegetables
3. dessert (Dessert often is cake or fruit.)

Words to Learn

Fruit

apple   banana   lemon   orange   peach   strawberry

Vegetables

tomato   lettuce   carrot   cucumber   potato   beans

Meat

chicken   hamburger   steak

Other Foods

bread   cake   cereal   cheese   egg   fish

pasta   rice   salad   sandwich   soup

Beverages

milk   juice

Meals/Parts of Meals

breakfast   lunch   dinner   dessert

YOU CAN ANSWER THESE QUESTIONS

Put an *x* in the box next to the correct answer.

Reading Comprehension

1. Every day, eat 2–4
   servings of
   ❑ meat.
   ❑ fruit.

2. Every day eat 3–5
   servings of
   ❑ sweets.
   ❑ vegetables.

3. Do not eat a lot of
   ❑ sweets.
   ❑ rice.

4. For bread, cereal,
   rice, and pasta eat
   ❑ 2–3 servings.
   ❑ 6–11 servings.

5. You eat breakfast
   in the
   ❑ morning.
   ❑ afternoon.

6. In the United States,
   most people eat
   ❑ three meals every day.
   ❑ one meal every day.

7. Dessert is often
   ❑ cake and fruit.
   ❑ lunch and dinner.

Vocabulary

8. Fruits include
   ❑ apples and cheese.
   ❑ oranges and bananas.

9. Vegetables include
   ❑ lettuce and tomato.
   ❑ lemon and cucumber.

10. Meat includes
    ❑ steak.
    ❑ bread.

How many questions did you answer correctly? Circle your
score. Then fill in your score on the Score Chart on page 91.

Number Correct	1	2	3	4	5	6	7	8	9	10
Score	10	20	30	40	50	60	70	80	90	100

EXERCISES TO HELP YOU

Exercise A
Practicing Vocabulary: Foods
Circle.

1. apple   chicken   fish

2. banana   tomato   bread

3. lettuce   cucumber   potato

4. orange   fish   cake

5. eggs   chicken   bananas

Exercise B
Practicing Vocabulary: Foods
Match.

1. cheese

2. soup

3. salad

4. pasta

5. sandwich

Exercise C
Practicing Vocabulary: More Food Words
Complete the sentences. Use words from the box.

apple	eggs
bananas	fish
bread	oranges
carrots	potatoes
chicken	tomatoes

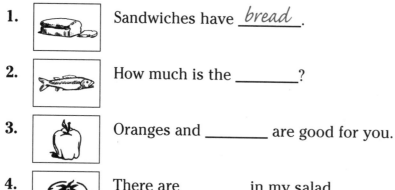

1. Sandwiches have _bread_ .

2. How much is the _____?

3. Oranges and _____ are good for you.

4. There are _____ in my salad.

5. I like _____ .

6. Many people like to eat meat and _____ .

7. Many people like juice from _____ .

8. You can have a _____ sandwich.

9. These _____ are on sale.

10. Potatoes and _____ are vegetables.

Exercise D
Practicing Vocabulary: Groups of Foods
Complete the pyramid.
Write the names of some foods.

Sweets and fats

Milk and _____

Meat, poultry,
fish, eggs

Vegetables

Fruit

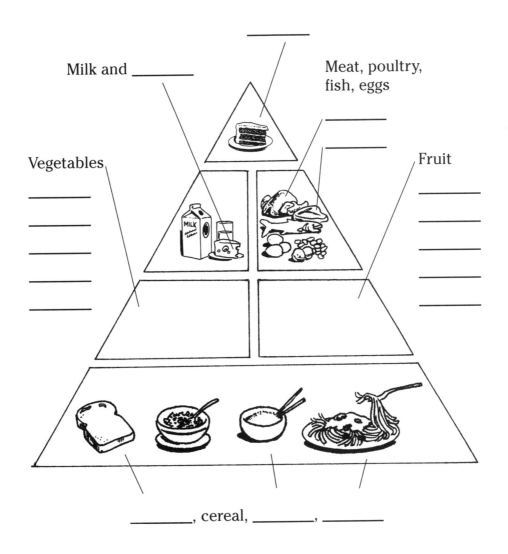

_____, cereal, _____, _____

Exercise E
Read and Write
Write the food groups.

Menu

The Pyramid Café

Soup
tomato soup
chicken soup with rice

Salads
lettuce and tomato salad
tomato and cucumber salad

Sandwiches
egg sandwich
hamburger

Meat
steak
chicken

Pasta
pasta with
tomato sauce

Side Dishes
potatoes
green beans

Beverages
milk
orange juice
carrot juice

Desserts
cake
apple pie
peach pie

---

1. orange juice   _____

2. apple   _____*fruit*_____

3. green beans   _____

4. hamburger   _____

5. cake   _____

Exercise F
Using Vocabulary
Look at the menu. Write a meal for yourself.

_____

_____

_____

_____

Try It
Read the conversation.

Work with a partner. Order your meal.

Sharing with Others

Part A

1. What are your favorite foods? Make a list.

_____   _____

_____   _____

_____   _____

_____   _____

2. Share your list with the class.

Part B

Interview a partner. Write your partner's favorite foods.

Partner's name: _____

_____   _____

_____   _____

Part C

Work with a partner. Look at your meal in Exercise F.
Write the food groups.

What food groups are in your meal? Is your meal good for you?

_____   _____

_____   _____

_____   _____

_____   _____

Unit 5

Invitations

Come to a picnic!

Who: Our Class
What: A Picnic
When: Saturday, May 12, 1:00 p.m.
Where: City Park

A Picnic in the Park

Come to a picnic!

Who: Our Class
What: A Picnic
When: Saturday, May 12, 1:00 p.m.
Where: City Park

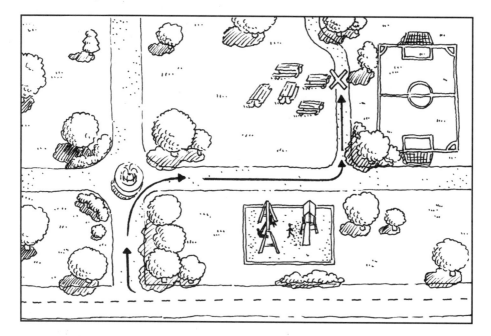

Come to City Park. Go to the Main Entrance.
Walk straight ahead to the fountain. Turn right.
Walk past the children's play area. Turn left.
Walk past the soccer field.
The picnic is in the picnic area.

Note:
Who = people
When = time
Where = place

Words to Learn

Directions

left
right
straight ahead

Actions

turn
walk

Places

park
soccer field
house
apartment building

Parties

picnic
birthday
graduation

Months of the Year

January
February
March
April
May
June
July
August
September
October
November
December

YOU CAN ANSWER THESE QUESTIONS

Put an *x* in the box next to the correct answer.

Reading Comprehension

1. What kind of party is it?
   - ❑ a birthday
   - ❑ picnic

2. *Who* in the invitation means
   - ❑ 1:00 p.m.
   - ❑ the class.

3. *Where* in the invitation means
   - ❑ the class.
   - ❑ the park.

4. *When* in the invitation means
   - ❑ 1:00 p.m.
   - ❑ the class.

5. Look at the directions. You go to the fountain. Then you
   - ❑ turn right.
   - ❑ turn left.

6. You go past the children's play area. Then you
   - ❑ turn right.
   - ❑ turn left.

7. You walk past the soccer field. Then you are at
   - ❑ the fountain.
   - ❑ the picnic area.

Vocabulary

8.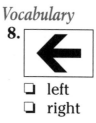
   - ❑ left
   - ❑ right

9.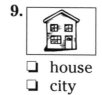
   - ❑ house
   - ❑ city

10.
    - ❑ birthday
    - ❑ picnic

How many questions did you answer correctly? Circle your score. Then fill in your score on the Score Chart on page 91.

Number Correct	1	2	3	4	5	6	7	8	9	10
Score	10	20	30	40	50	60	70	80	90	100

EXERCISES TO HELP YOU

Exercise A
Practicing Vocabulary: Question Words
Match.

1. Who   Dinner

2. What   Friday, September 10, 7:00 p.m.

3. When   Philip's house

4. Where   Students in our English class

Exercise B
Practicing Vocabulary: Question Words
Complete the invitation. Use the words in the box.

Who   Where   When   What

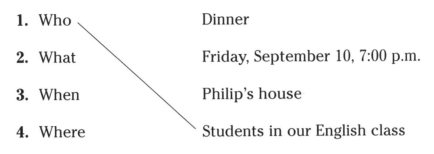

_____ : *Lila's friends and family*

_____ : *A Graduation Party*

_____ : *Lila's house*

_____ : *Sunday, June 12, 2:00 PM*

Exercise C
Practicing Vocabulary: Months
Write the names of the months.

January	Feb _ _ _ _ _ _	M _ _ _ _ _

_ _ _ _ _ _	M _ _	J _ _ _ _

_ _ _ _	_ _ _ _ _ _ _	Sept _ _ _ _ _ _

O _ _ _ _ _ _ _	November	D _ _ _ _ _ _ _ _

Circle the months. Write them in order on the lines below.

1. M R C A P R I L J U

2. N O F E B R U A R Y O

3. J A N P O C J U L Y

4. M A R C H M A J U N

5. S E P O C T O B E R N O

_____

_____

_____

_____

_____

Exercise D
Understanding Vocabulary: Directions
Read the directions. Circle.

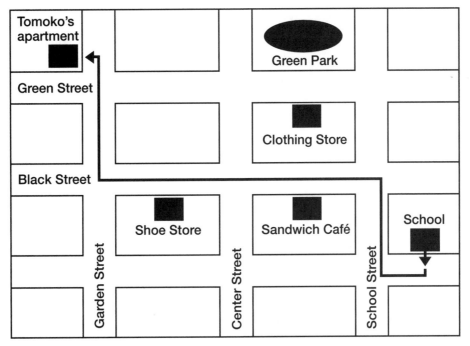

Juanita wants to go to Tomoko's apartment for dinner.

Juanita is at school.

1. Juanita turns right onto School Street.   (yes)   no

2. She turns left at Black Street.   yes   no

3. She goes straight ahead down Black Street.   yes   no

4. She goes past the Sandwich Café.   yes   no

5. She turns left at Garden Street.   yes   no

6. She goes past Green Park.   yes   no

7. Tomoko's apartment is on Green Street.   yes   no

Exercise E
Read and Write
Complete the invitation.

It's Dorothy's birthday. There's a birthday party for her.
Dorothy's friends are coming. The party is at Dorothy's house.
Her address is 375 Spring Street, Apartment 2B. The party is on
Saturday, March 12, at 7 p.m.

Who   :_____

What   :_____

When   :_____

Where :_____

Exercise F
Read and Write
Complete the directions to Dorothy's house.

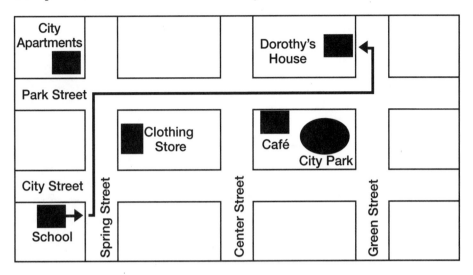

Go to the main entrance of the school.

Turn _____ onto Spring Street.

Go past the _____.

Turn _____ on Park Street.

Walk straight _____ down Park Street.

Go past the _____.

Turn left on _____ Street.

Dorothy's house is on your left.

Try It
Work with a partner. Give directions from Dorothy's house
to City Apartments.

SHARING WITH OTHERS

Part A

Write an invitation for a party at your house.

Who: _____

What: _____

When: _____

Where: _____

Part B

Share birth dates with the class. How many students were born in each month?

Part C

Work with a partner. Write directions from your school to a place. Draw a map.

_____

_____

_____

_____

_____

Unit 6

Health and Family

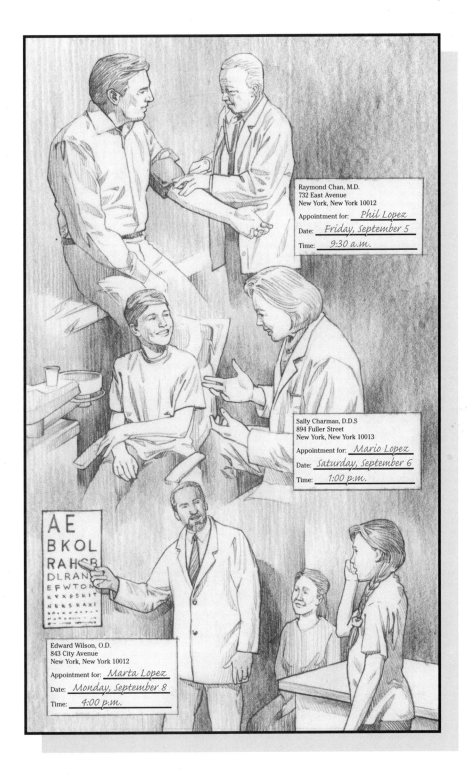

Raymond Chan, M.D.
732 East Avenue
New York, New York 10012

Appointment for: *Phil Lopez*

Date: *Friday, September 5*

Time: *9:30 a.m.*

Sally Charman, D.D.S
894 Fuller Street
New York, New York 10013

Appointment for: *Mario Lopez*

Date: *Saturday, September 6*

Time: *1:00 p.m.*

Edward Wilson, O.D.
843 City Avenue
New York, New York 10012

Appointment for: *Marta Lopez*

Date: *Monday, September 8*

Time: *4:00 p.m.*

Health Problems

Phil Lopez is sick. He has a cold.
He can look in a medical book for help.
For a bad cold, he can go to the doctor's office.

Medical Book
How to treat a cold

1. Stay in bed.

2. Drink liquids.

3. Take medicine like asprin.

Name ___Lopez, Phil_____

Date of Birth ___December 4, 1955_____

Reason for Visit ___Cold_____

Family History

Father   Name ___Martin_____ Age __75__

Check problems:
☒ heart problems   ❏ cancer   ❏ other

Mother   Name ___Maria_____ Age __74__

Check problems:
❏ heart problems   ❏ cancer   ❏ other

If you are married, complete this part.

Husband/Wife Name ___Elena_____ Age __41__

Children   Name ___Mario_____ Age __17__

                Name ___Marta_____ Age __13__

                Name ___Guadalupe_____ Age __10__

Words to Learn

Parts of the Body

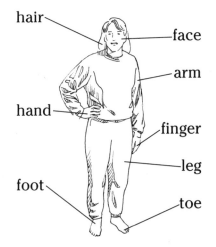

hair — face
arm
hand
finger
leg
foot
toe

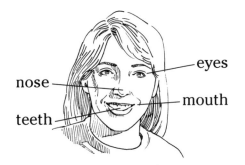

nose — eyes
mouth
teeth

Illnesses

cold

cough

runny nose

stomachache

headache

toothache

Doctors
doctor = M.D.
dentist = D.D.S.
eye doctor
    (optometrist) = O.D.

Other Words
appointment
checkup

YOU CAN ANSWER THESE QUESTIONS

Put an *x* in the box next to the correct answer.

Reading Comprehension

1. When you have a cold, it is a good idea to
   - ❏ stay in bed.
   - ❏ eat a lot.

2. When you have a cold,
   - ❏ do not eat or drink.
   - ❏ drink liquids.

3. Phil Lopez has a
   - ❏ bad cold.
   - ❏ heart problem.

4. Phil Lopez has an appointment with the
   - ❏ doctor.
   - ❏ dentist.

5. Phil Lopez has
   - ❏ four children.
   - ❏ three children.

6. Phil Lopez's father has
   - ❏ a heart problem.
   - ❏ cancer.

7. Phil Lopez's date of birth is
   - ❏ September 5, 1955.
   - ❏ December 4, 1955.

Vocabulary

8. When you have a problem with your teeth, you go to the
   - ❏ dentist.
   - ❏ optometrist.

9. When you have a problem with your eyes, you go to the
   - ❏ dentist.
   - ❏ optometrist.

10. When you have a cold, you go to the
    - ❏ dentist.
    - ❏ doctor.

How many questions did you answer correctly? Circle your score. Then fill in your score on the Score Chart on page 91.

Number Correct	1	2	3	4	5	6	7	8	9	10
Score	10	20	30	40	50	60	70	80	90	100

EXERCISES TO HELP YOU

Exercise A

Practicing Vocabulary: Parts of the Body

Write the parts of the body. Use the words in the box.

arm   face   finger   foot   hair   leg   toe   hand

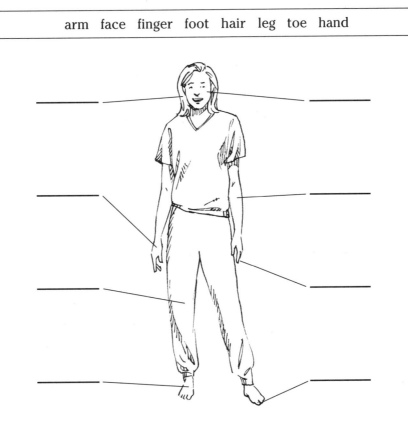

Write the parts of the face. Use the words in the box.

eyes   mouth   nose   teeth

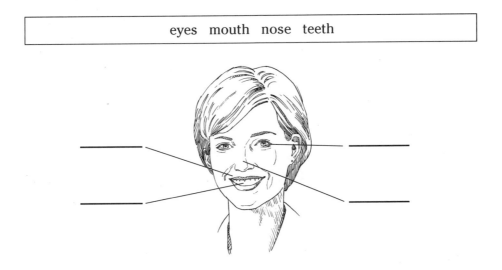

Exercise B
Practicing Vocabulary: Illnesses
Match.

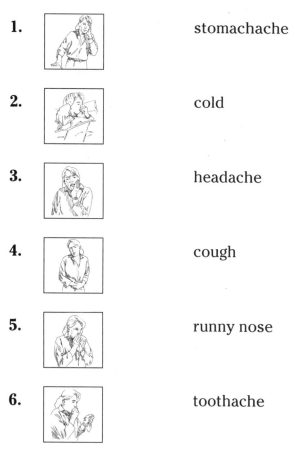

1. stomachache

2. cold

3. headache

4. cough

5. runny nose

6. toothache

Exercise C
Practicing Vocabulary: Illnesses
Complete the sentences. Use the words in the box.

cold   headache   stomachache   toothache

1. Inez ate a lot of sweets. Now she has a _____.

2. Ricardo is sick. He has a cough and runny nose.

    He has a _____.

3. Yoko has an appointment with the dentist.

    She has a _____.

4. Give me some aspirin. I have a _____.

Exercise D

Learning Vocabulary: Family Words

Read about Guadalupe Lopez's family.

Martin   Maria

Roberto   Rosa   Phil   Elena

Pedro   Mario   Marta   Guadalupe

Note: Parents = mother and father

Circle.

1. Elena is Guadalupe's mother.   (yes)   no

2. Martin is Guadalupe's grandfather.   yes   no

3. Rosa is Guadalupe's aunt.   yes   no

4. Mario is Guadalupe's brother.   yes   no

5. Marta is Guadalupe's cousin.   yes   no

6. Phil and Elena are Guadalupe's parents. yes   no

7. Roberto is Guadalupe's cousin.   yes   no

8. Pedro is Guadalupe's cousin.   yes   no

Exercise E
Practicing Vocabulary: Family Words
Write the family words in the correct column. Use the words in the box.

| mother brother son uncle wife |
| daughter father sister husband aunt |

Man	Woman
father	*mother*
_____	_____
_____	_____
_____	_____
_____	_____

Exercise F
Practicing Vocabulary: Family Words

1. Your mother's mother is your *grandmother* .

2. Your father's father is your _____.

3. Your father's sister is your _____.

4. Your mother's brother is your _____.

5. Your mother's husband is your _____.

6. Your aunt's son is your _____.

Try It
Work with a partner. Talk about Phil Lopez and his family. Use sentences like: "Phil's father is Martin."

Exercise G
Read and Write

My Family

My name is Takeshi. I live in the United States. But some of my family lives in Japan.

My father, Toshi, and my mother, Sachiko, were born in Japan. But they moved to the United States. My sister, Michiko, and I were born in the United States.

My father's parents still live in Japan. But I sometimes talk to my grandfather, Hiroshi, and to my grandmother, Keiko. We talk on the phone.

My father has one brother, Motoi. Motoi lives in the United States, too. Motoi and his wife, Suzy, have one daughter. Her name is Lena.

Complete Takeshi's family tree.

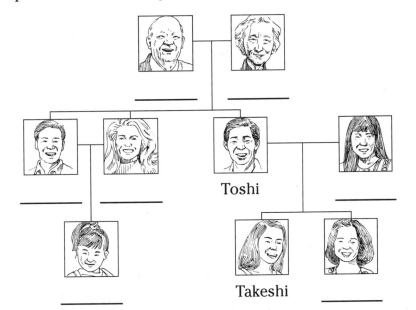

Toshi

Takeshi

SHARING WITH OTHERS

Part A

1. Draw your family tree.

2. Share your tree with a partner.

Part B

What do you do when you have a cold?
What do you do when you have a headache?

Tell a partner.

Unit 7

The Newspaper

The Newspaper

Today's Weather
Sunny and hot

Temperatures:
High in the 80s

Tomorrow's Weather
Morning:
Rainy and cool
Afternoon:
cloudy and cool.
The morning will be rainy,
but the rain will stop in
the afternoon.

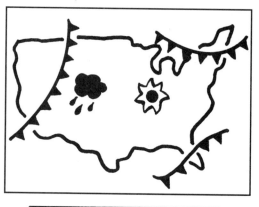

Weather for the Next Five Days:
Cool and sunny. High in 60s.

50,000 at Concert in the Park

Yesterday evening more than 50,000 people went to the free concert in the park. The large crowd of people heard music by the rock group, the Brothers and Sisters. It was the largest crowd in the history of the city.

The concert began at 7 o'clock in the evening, and it ended at 9 o'clock. The group played more than fifteen of their songs.

The weather was good. The temperature was in the 70s. It was warm and there was no rain.

"The music was good. I had a great time!" said Amy Childs, 18, one of the people at the concert.

"It was a great crowd," said Michael Speers of the Brothers and Sisters. "The people gave us a warm welcome."

Note: 50,000 = fifty thousand

Words to Learn

Weather

sunny   cloudy   rainy   snowy

Temperatures

cold   cool   warm hot

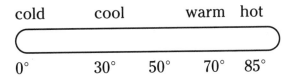

0°   30°   50°   70° 85°

Seasons

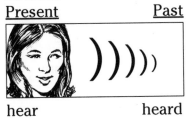
winter

spring

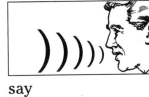
summer

fall

Time Words

yesterday	today	tomorrow
last (night)	now	next (week)
past	present	future

Actions

Present   Past   Present   Past

hear   heard   say   said

More Clothing Words

coat   raincoat   shorts   sunglasses   umbrella

YOU CAN ANSWER THESE QUESTIONS

Put an *x* in the box next to the correct answer.

Reading Comprehension
Look at the newspaper articles on page 72.

1. What is the weather like today?
   ❑ sunny and hot
   ❑ sunny and cold

2. What will the weather be tomorrow?
   ❑ rainy and cool
   ❑ sunny and cool

3. Where was the concert?
   ❑ at 7 o'clock
   ❑ at the park

4. When was the concert?
   ❑ at 7 o'clock
   ❑ the afternoon

5. What was the weather like at the concert?
   ❑ rainy
   ❑ warm

6. The number of people at the concert was
   ❑ 5,000
   ❑ 50,000

7. Who played at the concert?
   ❑ a rock group
   ❑ the crowd

Vocabulary

8.
   ❑ sunny
   ❑ cloudy

9. past
   ❑ yesterday
   ❑ today

10. future
    ❑ yesterday
    ❑ tomorrow

How many questions did you answer correctly? Circle your score. Then fill in your score on the Score Chart on page 91.

Number Correct	1	2	3	4	5	6	7	8	9	10
Score	10	20	30	40	50	60	70	80	90	100

EXERCISES TO HELP YOU

Exercise A
Practicing Vocabulary: Weather Words
Circle.

1. (sunny)   cloudy   (summer)

2. rainy   winter   snowy

3. fall   windy   cool

4. rainy   hot   spring

Exercise B
Practicing Vocabulary: Weather Words
Write about the weather for the seasons. Use the pictures in Exercise A for help.

1. In summer, it is ___*hot*___ and ___*sunny*___ .

2. In winter, it is _____ and _____ .

3. In fall, it is _____ and _____ .

4. In spring, it is _____ and _____ .

Exercise C
Practicing Vocabulary: Clothing
Match.

1. umbrella

2. raincoat

3. coat

4. sunglasses

5. shorts

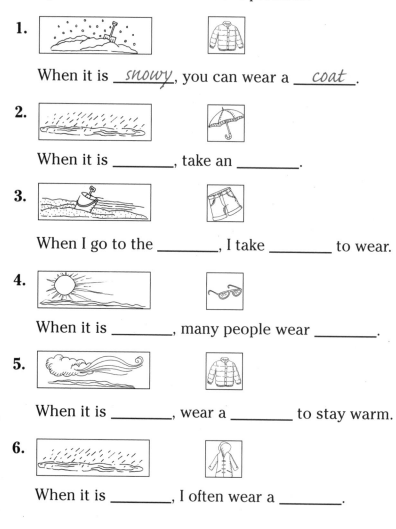

Exercise D
Practicing Vocabulary: Clothing and Weather
Complete the sentences. Use the pictures.

1. When it is ___*snowy*___, you can wear a ___*coat*___.

2. When it is _____, take an _____.

3. When I go to the _____, I take _____ to wear.

4. When it is _____, many people wear _____.

5. When it is _____, wear a _____ to stay warm.

6. When it is _____, I often wear a _____.

Exercise E
Understanding Vocabulary: Time Words
Circle.

		past	present	future
1.	today	past	(present)	future
2.	next week	past	present	future
3.	last night	past	present	future
4.	last Tuesday	past	present	future
5.	next Tuesday	past	present	future

Circle.

		past	present	future
1.	There was a concert last night.	past	present	future
2.	It will rain tomorrow.	past	present	future
3.	It is raining now.	past	present	future
4.	Next week there will be a soccer game.	past	present	future
5.	Yesterday it was hot.	past	present	future
6.	Today it is cool.	past	present	future

Read and Write
Look at the weather map.

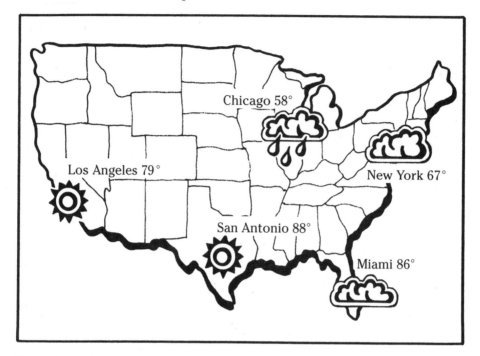

Complete the sentences.

1. In Los Angeles, the weather is __sunny__ and __warm__.

2. In Chicago, the weather is _____ and _____.

3. In New York, it is _____ and _____.

4. In Miami, it is _____ and _____.

5. In San Antonio, it is _____ and _____.

Try It
Work with a partner. Use the map. Tell about the weather in the cities.

Exercise G
Read and Write

**U.S. Will Play Brazil
in City Stadium**

A Large Crowd Will Fill Stadium

Next week two famous
soccer teams will come to
our city. The national
team of the United States
will play the national team
of Brazil.

City Stadium

Many soccer fans will come
to our city for the game.
More than 40,000 people
will be in City Stadium. It
will be the largest crowd in
the history of the stadium.

U.S. Team, Brazilian Team

The game is next Sunday
at 4:00 in the afternoon.
You can buy tickets for
the game at City Stadium.
The cost is $30.00 for one
ticket. There are about
5,000 tickets left.

---

1. What will happen? _A soccer game_

2. Who will play? _____

3. Who will come? _____

4. When will the game be? _____

5. Where will the game be? _____

6. How much money does a ticket cost? _____

SHARING WITH OTHERS

Part A

1. Work with a partner. What is the weather like today?

   _____

   _____

2. Work with a partner. What was the weather like yesterday?

   _____

   _____

3. Get a newspaper from your city. Work with a partner. What will the weather be like tomorrow?

   _____

   _____

Part B

1. What is the weather like in your native country?

   _____

   _____

2. Share with the class.

Unit 8

TV Listings

TV Listings

Channel 1

6:00 p.m. News
Channel 1 News at 6:00
Hear all the news from the city
and from around the world.

7:00 Talk Show
The Barbara Lane Show
The rock group Brothers and
Sisters are guests. They will
talk about their new songs.
The host is Barbara Lane.

8:00 Comedy
Phil's Problems
People remembered Phil's
birthday. But everybody gives
him the same present. He now
has 10 copies of the same CD.
What will he do? You will laugh.

9:00 Music Videos
The Newest Songs
All the newest songs from your
favorite music groups.

Channel 2

Cooking Show
Mario's Kitchen
How to make vegetable soup.
Mario gives his family's
recipe for vegetable soup.

Soap Opera
Life in the City
Three young women—Linda,
Sue, and Tina—share an
apartment. They also share
problems with money and
boyfriends. Today Linda
introduces her new boyfriend.
What's the problem? He was
Tina's boyfriend last year.

Drama
Dinosaurs!
A man goes back to the
time of the dinosaurs.

Sports
Basketball game
The Chicago Bulls play
the San Antonio Spurs.

Words to Learn

Kinds of TV Programs

news
comedy
drama
soap opera
commercial

Other TV Words

channel
TV program
TV show
watch TV

Time Words

before
after

9:00 a.m. ◄──── (10:00 a.m.) ────► 11:00

before 10:00   after 10:00

Other Words

boyfriend
girlfriend

cook   make food
recipe directions for making food
host   person who gives an invitation

CD

You can answer these questions

Put an *x* in the box next to the correct answer.

Reading Comprehension

1. What time is the news on TV?
   - ❑ 6:00 p.m.
   - ❑ 9:00 p.m.

2. What channel is the news on?
   - ❑ Channel 1
   - ❑ Channel 2

3. What program is on at 8:00?
   - ❑ *Phil's Problems*
   - ❑ *Music Videos*

4. What program is a soap opera?
   - ❑ *Life in the City*
   - ❑ *Dinosaurs!*

5. The drama at 8:00 is about
   - ❑ CDs.
   - ❑ dinosaurs.

6. The sports program at 9:00 is a
   - ❑ basketball game.
   - ❑ soccer game.

7. *Phil's Problems* is a
   - ❑ comedy.
   - ❑ drama.

8. The women in *Life in the City* have problems with
   - ❑ school.
   - ❑ boyfriends.

Vocabulary

9. 7:00 p.m. comes _____ 8:00 p.m.
   - ❑ before
   - ❑ after

10. 2:00 p.m. comes _____ 1:00 p.m.
    - ❑ before
    - ❑ after

How many questions did you answer correctly? Circle your score. Then fill in your score on the Score Chart on page 91.

Number Correct	1	2	3	4	5	6	7	8	9	10
Score	10	20	30	40	50	60	70	80	90	100

EXERCISES TO HELP YOU

Exercise A
Practicing Vocabulary: *Before, After*

Channel 1	Channel 4
4:00 Soap Opera *Boyfriends and Girlfriends*	News Comedy *City High Schools*
5:00 News	
6:00 Cooking Show How to make tomato sauce for pasta	Soccer Game The United States plays Canada.
7:00 Movie/Drama *A Doctor's Life*	Soccer Game—continued

Complete the sentences with *before* or *after*.

1. On Channel 1, there is a cooking show _____*after*_____
    the news.

2. On Channel 4, there is a comedy show _____
    the news.

3. On Channel 1, there is a soap opera _____ the news.

4. On Channel 4, there is a soccer game _____
    the comedy.

5. On Channel 1, there is a drama _____ the
    cooking show.

Try It
Work with a partner. Look at the TV listings in the newspaper.
Tell about the programs.

Exercise B
Read and Write

Channel 2

6:00 *News*
Richard Jones gives you the
news of the world and of
the city.

7:00 Comedy
Life in the Family
The parents and children
change places for a day.
The parents go to school.
The children go to work.
Who has the most problems?

8:00 Cooking Show
Adriana at Home
Adriana makes bread.

9:00 Drama
In Love
A young man in his 20s falls in
love with a woman in her 40s.
What will happen?

Channel 4

Soap Opera
Husbands and Wives
Fred meets his old girlfriend.
He takes her to lunch at a
café. Will Fred's wife find out?

Drama
Into the Future
A woman goes on a visit to
the future.

Movie Talk Show
Flora and Fred at the Movies
Flora and Fred talk about all
the new movies.

Sports
World Soccer

Read the conversation.

I watch TV most week nights. I like dramas and soap operas. I don't like sports, and I don't like programs where people sit and talk.

I watch TV about one night a week. I like to watch the news. I really like comedies, but I like sports the best.

What programs will Milva watch?

_____

_____

_____

What programs will Leo watch?

_____

_____

_____

Exercise C
What programs do you want to watch?

_____

_____

_____

Try It
Work with a partner. Tell about the kinds of TV shows you like.

Exercise D
Read.
Soap Operas

Many people like to watch soap operas on TV. Soap operas tell stories about families. They tell stories about people's personal lives. Usually the people in soap operas have problems.

Here is one story from a soap opera.

Ricardo came to the United States from Brazil last year. He is a student at City University. He studies art.

The first day at school Ricardo met Liliana. Liliana was also a new student. Liliana was also from Brazil. Ricardo liked to talk to Liliana about Brazil. They started to date. Liliana is now Ricardo's girlfriend.

This year Ricardo met Julie in his art class. Ricardo fell in love. He thinks Julie is beautiful. He likes to talk with her about art.

This year Liliana met Lou at the gym. She thinks Lou is handsome. He has big muscles. She likes to play sports with Lou. She likes Lou a lot.

Ricardo doesn't want to tell Liliana about Julie. He doesn't want to hurt her feelings.

Liliana doesn't want to tell Ricardo about Lou. She doesn't want to hurt his feelings.

One day they all meet on the street.

What will happen?

Watch the soap opera *City University* and find out.

Do you understand the story?
Circle.

1. Ricardo is from Brazil.   (yes)   no

2. Liliana is from the United States.   yes   no

3. Ricardo met Liliana this year.   yes   no

4. Liliana is now Ricardo's girlfriend.   yes   no

5. Ricardo met Julie in music class.   yes   no

6. Ricardo now loves Julie.   yes   no

7. Liliana met Lou at a gym.   yes   no

8. Liliana now likes Lou.   yes   no

9. Ricardo tells Liliana about Julie.   yes   no

SHARING WITH OTHERS

Part A

1. What are your favorite kinds of TV programs? Make a list.

   _____.

   _____.

   _____.

2. Share your list with a partner.

Part B

1. What kinds of TV programs do you watch? Write the kinds for each day for the next week.

Sunday	Monday	Tuesday	Wednesday	Thursday	Friday	Saturday

2. Share your list with the class. Which kinds of programs do most students like?

   _____.

   _____.

   _____.

Score Chart

This is the Score Chart for You Can Answer These Questions. Shade in your score for each unit. For example, if your score was 80 for **Letters and Numbers,** look at the bottom of the chart for **Letters and Numbers.** Shade in the bar up to the 80 mark. By looking at this chart, you can see how well you did on each unit.

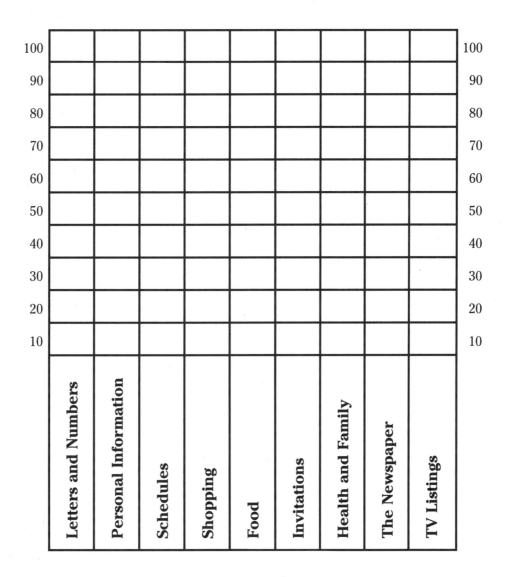